David Brent
SONGBOOK

Published by BLUE STREAK
an imprint of Weldon Owen
1045 Sansome Street, Suite 100
San Francisco, CA 94111

Weldon Owen is a division of Bonnier Publishing USA

Originally Published in 2016 by Blink Publishing in the United Kingdom

Library of Congress Cataloging in Publication data is available.

ISBN-10: 1-68188-183-7
ISBN-13: 978-1-68188-183-6

This Edition First Printed in 2016
10 9 8 7 6 5 4 3 2 1
2016 2017 2018 2019

Printed and bound by 1010 Printing in China

David Brent
SONGBOOK

BLUE STREAK

Contents

Introduction   9

Ooh La La   10

Native American   23

Lonely Cowboy   32

Freelove Freeway   45

Life on the Road   60

Slough   69

Thank Fuck It's Friday   83

Lady Gypsy   97

Please Don't Make Fun   110
of the Disableds

Paris Nights	119
Don't Cry It's Christmas	128
Spaceman	135
Equality Street	144
Ain't No Trouble	159
Electricity	173
Credits	190

INTRODUCTION

The songwriting in this book spans about 30 years. 'Freelove Freeway', 'Spaceman' and 'Equality Street', were written in the 1980s, whilst songs like 'Native American' and 'Electricity' were written in the last year. 'Equality Street' didn't have the rap back then, but that's what I do I guess. I bring already timeless works of art up to date and make them as relevant as ever.

But don't take my word for it. Just take a look at this photo of me and Dom Johnson (mixed-race rapper). That's what I'm talking about, really. Evolution. Who'd have thought back in the 1980s when I first started out in the rock and roll game that 30 years later I would still be at the cutting edge of music and passing on my musical wisdom and trailblazing attitude to a new generation?

Enjoy learning and playing these songs and putting your own spin on them. They were all written on an acoustic guitar but will probably sound great on any instrument. Except, maybe a trombone. But nothing sounds good on a trombone. I can't imagine why anyone would choose that as their instrument. Weird.

Ooh La La

The title is already a bit sexy and the rest of the song doesn't disappoint. It's about me driving across America to Mexico picking up chicks on the way. Write about what you know. And I know I would love to do that, one day. Not in a sexist way. Consensual. And safe. I will always use a condom, even if the woman says she's on the pill. I'm like, "I don't care luv, what about VD?" Also, I get condoms for free as I work for Lavichem (one of the biggest distributors for toilet vending machines in the UK), so even if the sex is disappointing it's not like it's cost me anything.

Don't get me wrong, I will wine and dine a lady, but if she's suddenly all, "Ooh lets have champagne, let's have desserts, let's have brandy..." I'm like "Oh, are we going halves?" That usually shuts 'em up. #NotAMug.

Ooh La La

Sold my shack in Memphis
Bought me a Chevrolet
Six string in the back
And a bottle of Jack
And I headed down to Mexico Way

Chorus

Singing Ooh la la la
Ooh la la la la lay
Ooh la la la la la la la
It's a beautiful day

Well I picked up this señorita
She was sitting in the golden hay
She said "I do not speak the English"
I said "Baby, there's nothing that you need to say,
I can see that we're going the same way..."

Chorus

Well, we rolled into Acapulco
And we sat in the desert sun
I played my guitar
And I smoked a cigar
And I said this is where I move on
Sure she cried but by then I was gone

Chorus

Ooh la la la
Ooh la la la la lay
Ooh la la la la la la la
It's a beautiful day
Oh, it's a beautiful day
Yeah, it's a beautiful day

Ooh La La

Words and Music by
David Brent

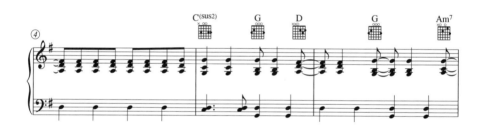

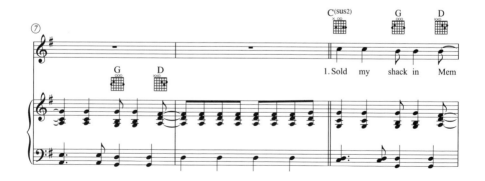

-phis, bought_ me a Che -v(a)-ro - let,_____ six_

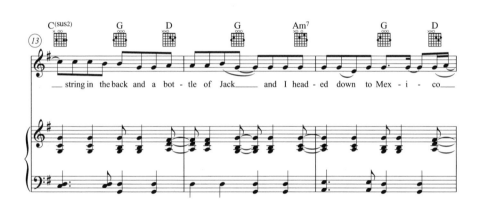

_string in the back and a bot - tle of Jack___ and I head - ed down to Mex - i - co___

_ Way. Sing - ing "Ooh_____ la, la,____ la, ooh,

la,— la, la, la, lay,— ooh———————— la, la,

la, la,— la, la, la, it's— a beau - ti - ful— day."

2. Well,— I picked up this se - ño - ri -

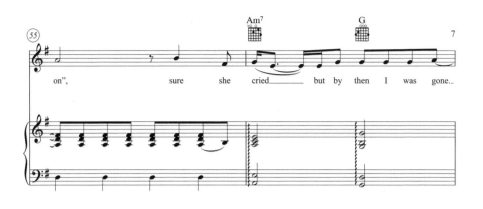

on",   sure   she   cried_____ but by then I was gone.__

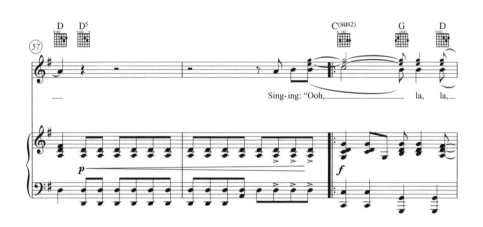

__   Sing-ing: "Ooh,_____ la,   la,__

__ la,   ooh,___ la,__ la, la, la, lay,__

ooh_____ la, la,____ la, la,___ la, la, la, it's__ a beau-ti - ful__

(Sing 2nd time)

__ day, (oh,)_____ it's__ a beau - ti - ful_____ day, yeah,_____
(It's a beau - ti - ful__

__ it's__ a beau-ti - ful_____ day.
__ day.)

Native American

Typical me. Getting political. I just think it's about time someone said something. Sue me. This song is about the plight of the Native American and how the white man came and stole their land and put them into reservations and worse (killed them). It's very hard-hitting but still poetic with wonderful imagery. That's sort of what I do.

"Oh your red heart rages. Cut down, burned out and put in cages." I've said they're angry and got the word "red" in there to symbolise passion and a beating heart that won't give up. It's not because they used to be called Red Indians, because, as the song explains, they don't like being called that any more. It also explains why. So... informative. I also love how I use the word cages instead of reservations. Powerful. (Also, it rhymes with "rages". Perfect.) I didn't mention how they've sort of had the last laugh, as they can do what they like now on those reservations (gambling etc.), because it sort of goes against my original point. But good luck to them.

Native American

Oh, your red heart rages.
Cut down, burned out and put in cages
You came in peace held up your hand, "How!"
We cut it off and we stole your land

Oh Native American
Soar like an eagle sit like a Pelican
Oh don't call us Indians
We're more like west Eurasians
Crossed with Siberians

White man's eyes too blind to see
A gentle race so wild and free
They called you savages,
Called you bad
But the scalping thing
Was only when you got real mad.

Oh Native American
Soar like an eagle sit like a Pelican
Oh, don't call us Indians
We're more like west Eurasians
Crossed with Siberians

Oh Native American
Soar like an eagle sit like a Pelican
Oh don't call us Indians
We're more like west Eurasians
Crossed with Siberians

Native American

Words and Music by
David Brent

1. Oh,_____ your red__heart rag es, cut down, burned out and put in cag
2. White man's eyes too blind to see a gent-le race so wild and

- es, you came in peace, held up your hand,___ "How!"
___free. They called you savag-es, called you bad,___ but the

Lonely Cowboy

The music is in the style of cool country and western but the lyrics conjure brilliant imagery. It's about a guy in the "wilderness" who thought his woman was an angel but turned out to be a winged demon. Not literally. It's metaphorical. Although, in the video I think Dom and I would be dressed as actual cowboys to drive home the point. And before you say "Why would someone like Dom have been in the Wild West?" I checked on Wikipedia and there were some. So, factually accurate, again.

Lonely Cowboy

You blew into town like a hurricane,
Dust cloud cleared and you were
there one day
Well I don't remember praying for a miracle,
But I prayed that you would never
go away.

I thought you were my guardian angel,
I thought your wings would keep me
warm and dry,
But you pecked me to the bone, and
you left me here alone,
And you spread your wings and flew
into the sky.

Now what you know about the wilderness
What you know about lassoin a bear in the face
Or how to kill a fish
How to skin and fillet it?
Listen to what I'm dealing with
There ain't no hood in the world
That gets as real as this.
You can munch your sandwich up
brother my hunter gatherer, battling
up a scavenger's might have to
punch a challenger, damage a hyena,
vultures and all, don't think I
won't kick a wolf in the balls,
I'm a loner, roaming alone I gotta

be ready for anything even though
my heart's been heavy since she
left me, and she can kiss my
horse's arse, yeah I'm lonely now
but I'm the lonely cowboy she's
just a lonely cow and now these
plains are my house, she'll never
spoil it, ground's my lounge, lakes
my bath, woods are my toilet,
rolling stones trust me, dusty roads
are where my home's at, a man
among the mountains but nothing
like Brokeback

Now I'm just a lost and lonely cowboy
Stripped and burned out on this
dusty plain
And God's mysterious ways ain't
welcome here today,
Cos there ain't no soul to save
just flesh and pain
Yeah there ain't no soul to save
just flesh and pain

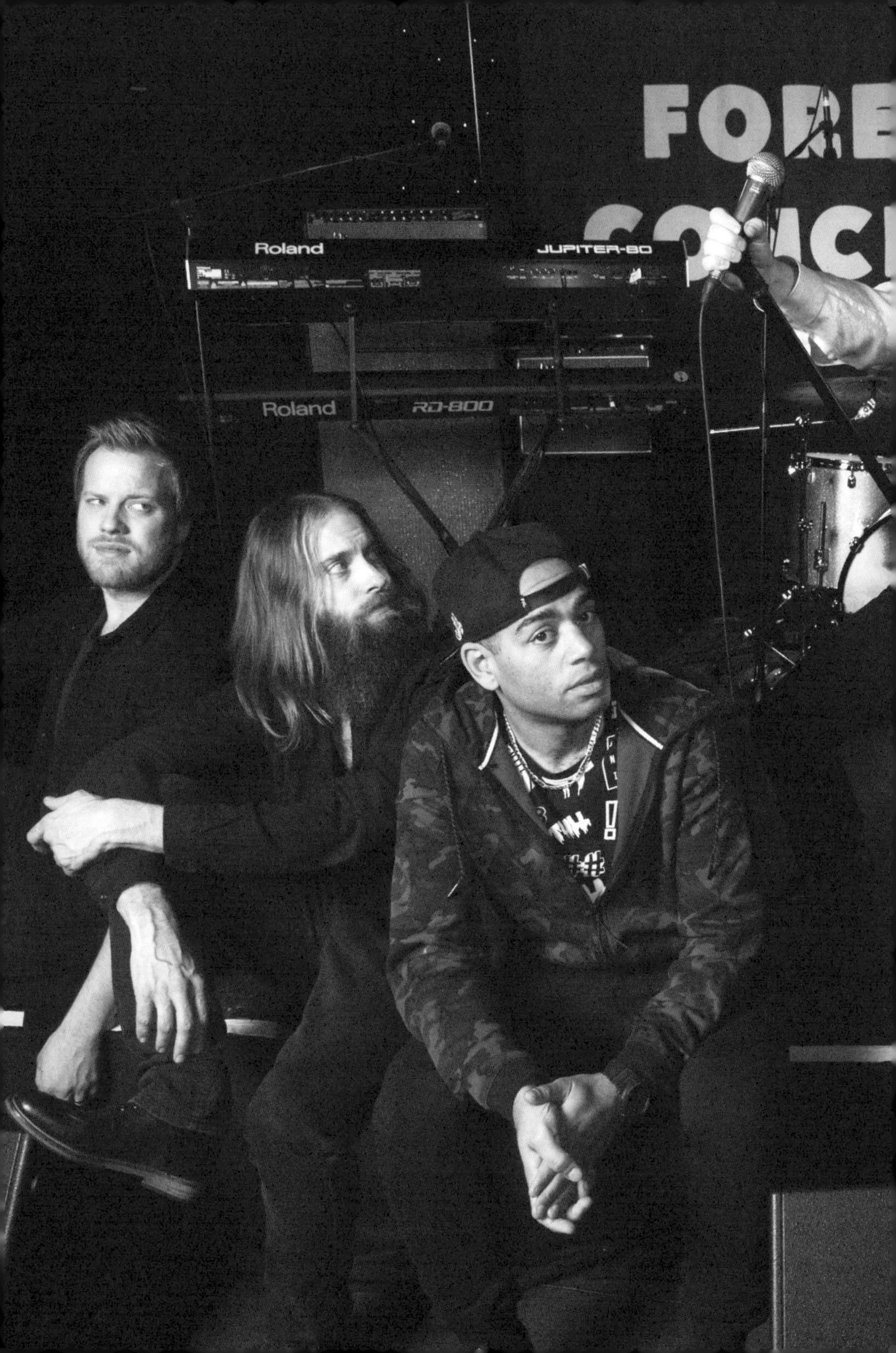
Roland
JUPITER-80
Roland
RD-800

Lonely Cowboy

Words and Music by David Brent
Rap by Dom Johnson

Well, I don't___ re - mem - ber pray - ing for___ a mi -
But you pecked___ me to the bone and you left___
And___ God's myst - er - ious ways___ ain't wel

rac - le, but I prayed___ that you___ would
___ me here___ a - lone___ and you spread___ your wings_ and
- come here___ to - day,___ 'coz there ain't___ no soul___ to save,

Coda ⊕

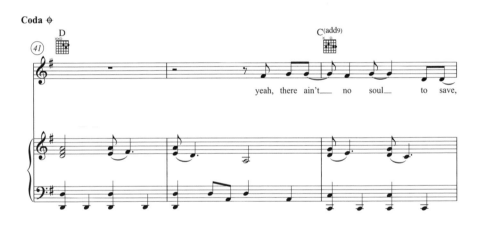

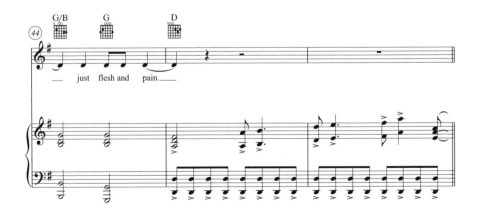

6

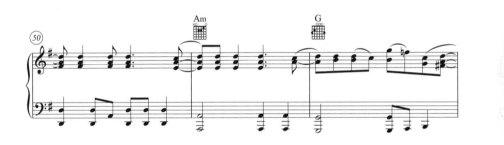

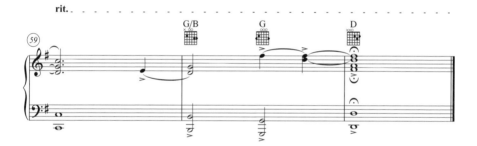

Freelove Freeway

This is one of the first songs I wrote with the original line up of Foregone Conclusion back in the mid 1980s. It hasn't dated at all, to be honest. It's got my favourite four chords of all time in my favourite order, too. C, F, Am, G, over and over again. This makes it very catchy and allows you to concentrate on the story being played out in the lyrics. Clever.

Freelove Freeway

Pretty girl on the hood of a
Cadillac, yeah.
She's broken down on Freeway Nine
I take a look and get her engine started
Leave her purring and I roll on by
Bye bye

Free love on the free love freeway,
The love is free and the freeway's long
I got some hot love on the hot love highway
Ain't going home because my baby's gone
She's gone

Little while later see a señorita
She's caught a flat trying to make it home
She says, por favour can you pump me up?
I said, muchos gracias and adios.
Bye bye

Free love on the free love freeway
The love is free and the freeway's long
I got some hot love on the hot love highway
Ain't going home cos my baby's gone
She's gone

Down the road, I see a cowboy crying
Hey buddy, what can I do?
He said, I led a good life, I had
about a thousand women
I said then why the tears? He said
Cos none of them was you...

Free love on the free love freeway
The love is free and the freeway's long
I got some hot love on the hot love highway
Ain't going home cos my baby's gone
She's gone
Free love on the free love freeway
The love is free and the freeway's long
I got some hot love on the hot love highway
Ain't going home coz my baby's gone
She's gone
She's gone
She's gone
She's gone

Freelove Freeway

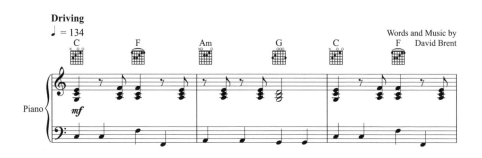

Driving

♩ = 134

Words and Music by
David Brent

Piano

1.Pret - ty girl on the hood of a Cad-il-lac yeah.
2.Lit - tle while la - ter see a señ - or - ita.

She's bro - ken down on___ Free - way Ni - ne.
She's caught a flat try'n - a make it___ home. She says___

I take a look and get her
"Por fa - vor___ can you

go - ing home___ be - cause my ba - by's gone.___ She's gone___

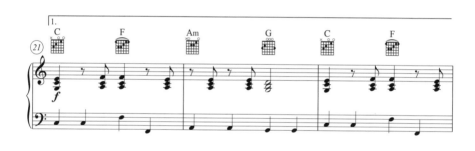

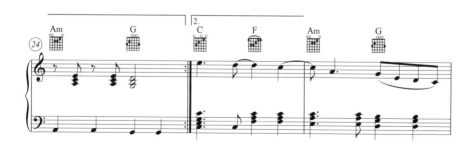

4

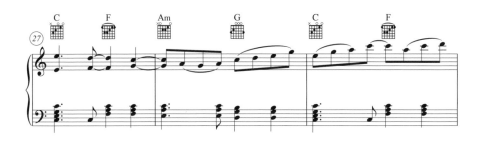

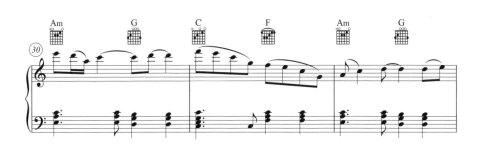

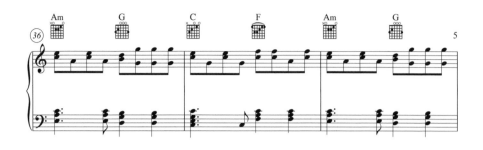

Down the road__ I see a cow-boy cry-ing

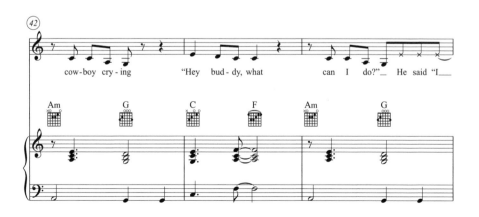

"Hey bud - dy, what can I do?"__ He said "I__

led a good life, I had a-bout a thou-sand wo-men." I said "Then why the tears?" He said "'Cos

none of them was you." Free love on the free love free - way, the

love is free and the free - way's long. I got some hot love on the

hot love high-way, ain't go-ing home coz my ba-by's gone. She's gone!_

She's gone!_ She's gone!_

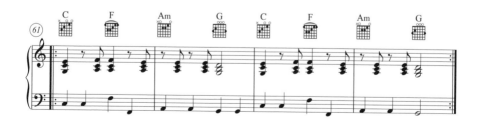

Life on the Road

This is the song they chose as the title track to the documentary. When I agreed to do it I suggested various titles, but they didn't go with any of them. I can't believe they didn't like 'Bantman Returns' but they know best (not! LOL).

I pointed out that 'Life on the Road' was about me repping. Not about touring. They said "Yeah, that's why it's funny." I've no idea what they meant. Anyway, the lyrics say it all. It not only beautifully captures how exciting selling cleaning products can be, but it specifically mentions some of the places I visit and makes everything rhyme.

That's songwriting.

Life on the Road

Half a tank should get me to Millbank
I fill her up and head down to Sidcup
It's just a meeting
It's only fleeting
It's just a pitch
And then I'm up to Ipswich

Life on the road
Don't need a heavy load
Foot down to the floor
70 miles an hour
But no more

Wheeler dealing, no feeling
Strictly business, I'm killin' it
in Widnes
Then to Gloucester
I get a Costa.
Hard shoulder?
Coffee holder

Life on the road
Don't need a heavy load
Foot down to the floor
70 miles an hour
But never more

(Repeat Chorus 1)

(Repeat Chorus 2)

Life on the Road

Words and Music by
David Brent

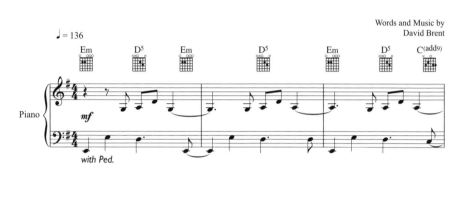

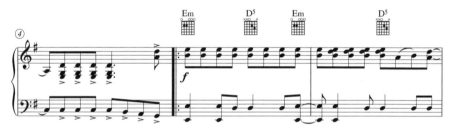

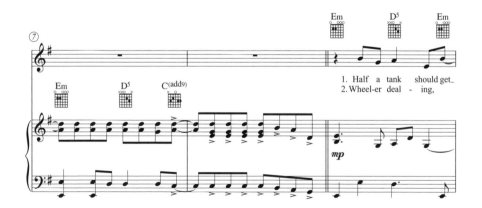

1. Half a tank should get_
2. Wheel-er deal - ing,

don't need a heav-y load,___ foot down___ to the floor,

1.
se-ven-ty___ miles an hour,___ but no___ more.

2.
se-ven-ty miles an hour,___ but ne-ver more.

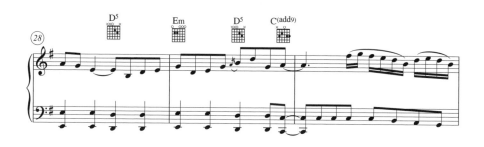

Life on the road,___

Slough

The reason I wrote this song is that, to me, Slough is the best place in the world, and I was tired of people like John Betjeman dissing it. I'd love to have seen him come here and say all that shit to our faces. He would have got a slap. When he was younger, I mean. Not when he was old and in a wheelchair. We don't hit the crippled, however annoying they are. It's just not how we do things round here. Anyway, everything in the song is factually accurate, so not only is it a beautiful tune but it's educational too.

Slough

More convenient than a Tesco Express
Close to Windsor but the property's less
It keeps the businesses of Britain great
It's got Europe's biggest trading estate
It doesn't matter where you're from
You wanna work? Then come along
The station's just got a new floor
And the motorway runs by your door

And you know just where you're headin'
It's equidistant 'tween London and Readin'

Oh, Slough,
My kinda town
I don't know how
Anyone could put you down
Oh Slough
My kinda town
I don't know how
Anyone could put you down

To the west you've got Taplow and Bray
You've got Hillingdon the other way
It's a brilliant place to live and work
It was in Bucks now officially it's Berks
Don't believe what the critics say
Like "it's soulless and boring and grey"
See for yourself, what you waiting for?
We're on the Bath Road, that's the A4

And you know just where you're headin'
It's equidistant 'tween London and Readin'

Oh Slough
My kinda town
I don't know how
Anyone could put you down
Oh Slough
My kinda town
I don't know how
Anyone could put you down

And you know just where you're headin'
It's equidistant 'tween London and Readin'

Oh Slough
My kinda town
I don't know how
Anyone could put you down
Oh Slough
My kinda town
I don't know how
Anyone could put you down

Slough
Slough
Slough
Oh Slough

Slough

Words and Music by
David Brent

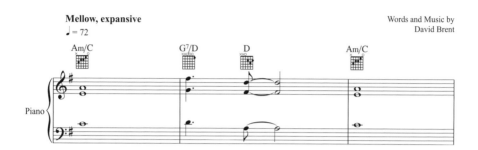

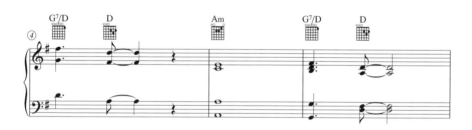

More con -1.ven - ient than a Tes - co Ex - press,   close to
To the 2.west you've got__ Tap-low and Bray,   you've got

Wind-sor but the prop-er-ty's less.
Hill-ing-don the o-ther_ way.
It keeps the busi-ness-es of Bri-tain great, it's got
It's a brill-iant place to live and_ work, it was in

D *C* *Em* *G*

Eu-rope's big-gest tra-ding es-tate.
Bucks now of-fic-ial-ly it's Berks.
It does-n't mat-ter where you're from; you wan-na
Don't be-lieve_ what the cri-tics_ say, like "it's

D *C* *Em* *G*

work? Then come a-long.
soul-less and bo-ring and grey".
The sta-tion's just got a new floor and the
See for your-self, what you wai-ting for? We're on the

D *C* *Em* *G*

mo-tor-way runs by your door. And you know just where you're head-in' It's e-qui-
Bath road, that's the A 4.

dis-tant 'tween Lon-don and Rea- din'. Oh, Slough,

my kind of town, I don't know how a-ny-one could put you down. Oh,

4

Slough,_____ my kind-a town, I don't know how_____

Am   G   D   Am

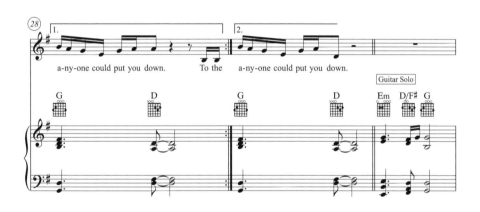

1.
a-ny-one could put you down. To the

2.
a-ny-one could put you down.

Guitar Solo

G   D   G   D   Em D/F# G

D   C   Em D/F# G   D   C

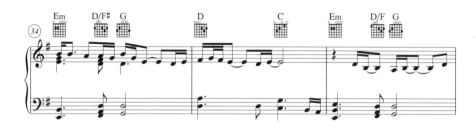

And you know just where you're head- in', it's e-qui

dis-tant 'tween Lon-don and Rea- din'. Oh,_____ Slough,_____

6

my kind-a town, I don't know how_____ a-ny-one could put you down. Oh,_____

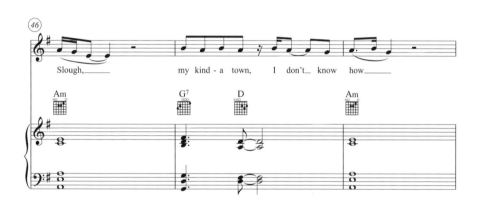

Slough,_____ my kind - a town, I don't_ know how_____

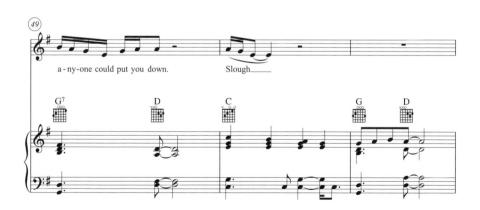

a - ny-one could put you down. Slough_____

Thank Fuck It's Friday

This is a song about how, wherever I am in the country, selling cleaning products, I always make it back to Slough for the weekend. It has a Rolling Stones vibe to it, which really works when you think about it.

I'm sort of a Rolling Stone, gathering no moss, etc. I'm always moving. Up and down the country, I mean. Not moving house or moving away from Slough or anything. No point. Slough's got everything I need. But I also like to travel and see the rest of the world. I've got clients in London, Gloucestershire, Wiltshire, Dorset, Essex and Kent. Suffolk, Cambridgeshire, Norfolk. You name it. I've even got quite a big client in Lincolnshire so I really do travel, boy.

Thank Fuck It's Friday

I work so hard just to pay my bills
I play even harder, yeah life kills
Now I'm burnin' rubber on the M25
Got a crazy weekend. Some of us
won't make it out alive.

Cuz this is my day
Thank Fuck it's Friday
Yeah this is my day
Thank Fuck it's Friday

I wake up Sunday feeling Saturday pain,
Dry Cleaners, 5 white shirts,
on the road again.
A week in cheap motels, yeah
I'm earning my bread
As long as I'm back for the weekend,
Hey, I'll sleep when I'm dead

Cuz this is my day
Thank Fuck it's Friday
Yeah this is my day
Thank Fuck it's Friday

This is my day
Thank Fuck it's Friday
Yeah this is my day
Thank Fuck it's Friday
This is my day
Thank Fuck it's Friday
Yeah this is my day
Thank Fuck it's Friday
My day
Thank Fuck it's Friday
Yeah this is my day

Thank Fuck it's Friday
Thank Fuck it's Friday
Thank Fuck it's Friday
Thank Fuck it's Friday
Thank Fuck it's Friday

Thank Fuck It's Friday

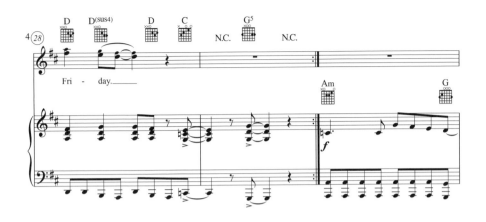

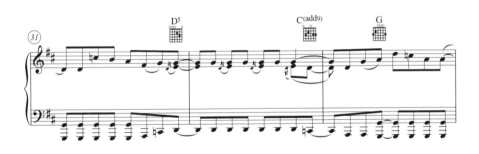

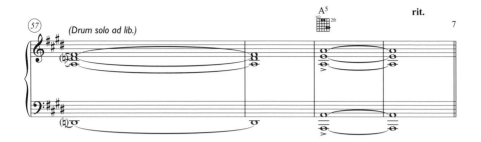

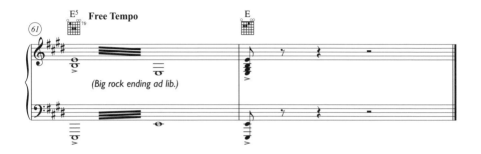

3

Lady Gypsy

This is a beautiful folk ballad about young love. First love, actually. It's about the time I lost my virginity to a Gypsy. A lady Gypsy, obviously. Hence the title. She was beautiful. Probably still is. Although, she'd be in her late fifties now, so I bet her tattoos are a right mess, due to saggage. Still, good luck to her. Although, she probably doesn't need luck with all the heather she handles.

Lady Gypsy

When I had known only 18 summers
I headed west through the Whitley Wood
To make my fortune and find a lover
And to lead the best life a young man could

Lai lai lai lai lai lai lai,
Oh lai lai lai lai lai lai lai lai lai.

And by the lakeside, just south of Didcot
I spied an angel, just standing there
She was a traveller, but she was pretty
And clean, she was in the water washing her hair

I lost my heart to a lady Gypsy
So long ago I forget her name
But I still remember the smell of the flowers
And the way my life would never be the same.

She laid me down on a bed of heather
She said "Please be careful this is what I sell"
I said "You're a hooker?"
She said "No I mean the heather.
I sell the heather, like a lucky spell."
I said "But to be clear then, the sex is free, yes?"
She said "Yes the sex is free. The heather's a pound"
I said "I don't need no heather and if I did
I would just pick some. It's free.
It's growing in the ground"

I lost my heart to a lady Gypsy
So long ago I forget her name
But I still remember the smell of the flowers
And the way my life would never be the same.

I lost my heart to a lady Gypsy
So long ago I forget her name
But I still remember the smell of the flowers
And the way my life would never be the same

When I had known only 18 summers...

Lady Gypsy

Words and Music by
David Brent

Folk ballad

♩ = 100

Piano

mf

When I___ had known on - ly eigh - teen sum - mers,
And by___ the lake - side,___ just south of Did - cot,

I head - ed west through the Whit - ley___ wood to make my for - tune and
I spied an an - gel, just stand - ing___ there. She was___ a trav' ler, but

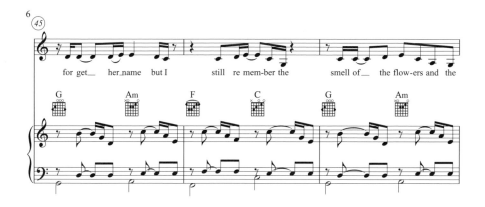

for get__ her_name but I   still re mem-ber the   smell of__ the flow-ers and the

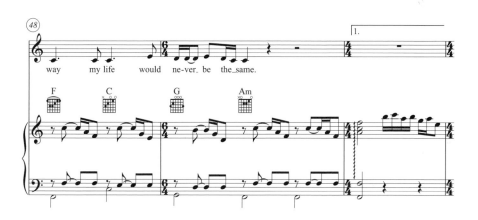

way   my life   would   ne-ver_ be   the_same.

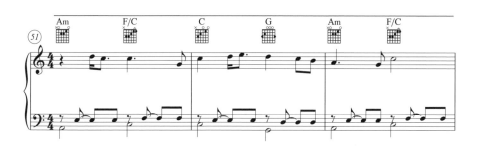

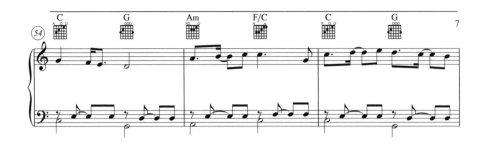

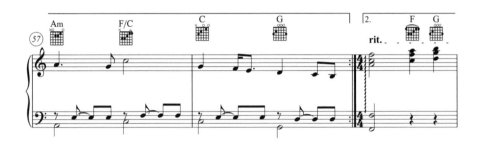

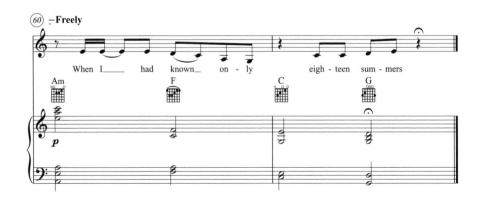

When I____ had known____ on - ly eigh - teen sum - mers

Please Don't Make Fun of the Disableds

People often say to me, "David, you're an entertainer and a great comedic mind, but is there anything you won't make a joke about?" And I always say, "Yes. The Handicapped." I will not laugh at them, or with them. Just to be safe. There's nothing funny about them and you might get in trouble, too. And this song is sort of a warning about all that.

I haven't listed every disability as I didn't want the song to be too depressing, but I've certainly touched on some of the big ones. I didn't bother with dwarves, for example, as we cover that in 'Equality Street'. Likewise, blindness gets a mention in 'Ain't No Trouble' and 'Don't Cry It's Christmas', so they should be well happy. (I've never given the deaf a shout-out in a song as there's not much point.)

Please Don't Make Fun of the Disableds

Oh please don't make fun of the disableds
There's nothing funny about those
Whether mental in the head or
Mental in the legs,
Doesn't mean their sorrow doesn't show
Oh no no no,

Please don't make fun of the disableds
Or you might get fired
The ones who cannot walk
The ones who cannot talk
Even the ones with ME who feel tired
We all feel tired,
Sometimes we all feel tired,

Please be kind to the ones with feeble minds,
Help the awkward through a door
Hold their hand if they've got one
Understand you might have to feed
The worst ones through a straw.

It's basically a head on a pillow

Ooooh please don't make fun of the disableds
There's nothing funny about those
Whether mental in the head or
Mental in the legs,
Doesn't mean their sorrow doesn't show
Oh no no, nooo,
Oh no no, nooo.

Please Don't Make Fun of the Disableds

Words and Music by
David Brent

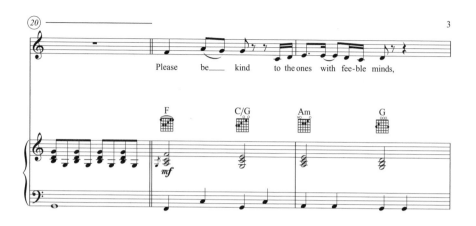

It's bas-ic-ally a head on a pil-low. (Head on a pil-low, head on a pil-low) Oh_

please don't make fun of the di - sa - bleds, there's no-thing fun - ny ab-out

those. Whe-ther men-tal in the head or men - tal in the legs, does-n't mean

Paris Nights

You may have heard a bit of this in *The Office* when I was singing it to Dawn to cheer her up. But she was all like, "Ooh, was that originally about Princess Diana?" Yes, Dawn, it was, but now you've interrupted me so no one got to hear the second verse. And it's the second verse where some of the most powerful imagery and insightful messages are. The guitar solo sort of represents the tragic car chase, by the way. Clever. And sad, obviously.

Paris Nights

A rose you never used your thorns
The ones you loved abandoned you
Your angel face made hearts a warm
You helped the sick but who helped you?
Then rushing through the Paris night
They hounded you, you lost control
We prayed that you would be alright
The news came through, your body cold

Goodnight my sweet princess
Sleep tight my sweet princess

The Queen of Hearts you used your power
To comfort those in their darkest hour
You hugged a man with full-blown AIDS
To show the world you can't catch it that way
It's only spread via blood
By sharing needles that are infected
Another way is having anal sex with
strangers unprotected

Goodnight my sweet princess
Sleep tight my sweet princess

Goodnight my sweet princess
Sleep tight my sweet princess

Goodnight my sweet princess
Sleep tight my sweet princess

Goodnight my sweet princess
Sleep tight my sweet princess

Paris Nights

Good - night, my sweet princ - ess, sleep tight, my sweet princ -

ess. 2. The Good - night, my sweet princ -

ess, sleep tight, my sweet princ - ess.

Don't Cry It's Christmas

This is a tear-jerker and a true story. It's about a little orphan kid I read about in the *Bucks Gazette* a few years ago. He was dying in a hospital in Slough and just wanted to stay alive till Christmas to meet Santa. This imagines me singing to him and telling him everything will be okay. It would have made a great video for a charity single. Unfortunately, I never did get to actually sing it to him as he went to a better place. A children's hospice in Ealing. Where he died.

Hopefully there will be others in the same position I can sing it to though. I never give up hope.

Don't Cry It's Christmas

Don't cry, it's Christmas,
Santa's coming soon,
Though you ain't got a mummy or daddy,
Santa still loves you,
And he's riding on his reindeer
To trample down the gloom
So don't cry, it's Christmas
Santa's coming soon

Don't cry, it's Christmas,
Santa's feeling fine,
Though you know you'll never see him,
He's not just in your mind,
And it's not that he's invisible
It's because you're going blind,
But don't cry it's Christmas
Santa's feeing fine.

Don't cry, it's Christmas,
Santa's on his way,
Though he's got a billion children,
He's only got one day,
You've got slightly less than that,
If I were you I'd pray,
But don't cry it's Christmas,
Everything's okay

Ooohhhhh, it's Christmas
Ooohhhhh, it's Christmas
Ooohhhhh, it's Christmas
OOohhhhh, it's Christmas
OOohhhhh, it's Christmas
OOohhhhh, it's Christmas
OOohhhhh, it's Christmas
OOohhhhh, it's Christmas

Don't Cry It's Christmas

Words and Music by
David Brent

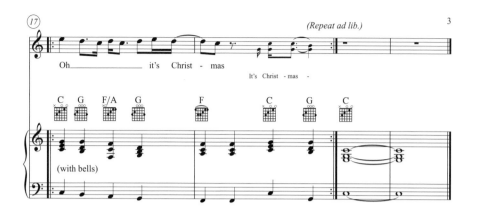

(Repeat ad lib.)

Oh_____ it's Christ - mas

It's Christ - mas -

(with bells)

Spaceman

This is a brilliantly poetic and socio-political song about race and religion as seen through the eyes of an alien. What would a more intelligent being think of our silly prejudices? And could he cure them? Yes. He does in the song anyway. I love how I've used the word "cure" there. It suggests that racism is a disease. Not like the mumps or AIDS, obviously, but I like to think we will end all prejudice one day and all humans will live as one. That way, if aliens did invade and they were trying to change us too much, we would band together and destroy them.

Spaceman

Spaceman came down to answer some things
The world gathered round from paupers to kings
I'll answer your questions, I'll answer them true
I'll show you the way, you'll know what to do
Who is wrong and who is right?
Yellow, brown, black or white?
The Spaceman he answered "You'll no longer mind
I've opened your eyes. You're now colour-blind"

The Spaceman looked human but with black shiny eyes
He spoke brilliant English, his voice synthesised
He travelled the country just spreading the word
Of love and affection, he picked up a bird
The bird it was dead but he made it just fine
He walked on the water and turned it to wine
A young child he said "Are you Christ in a mask?"
"No I'm just magic but I can see why you'd ask"

Space man came down (Spaceman)
Space man came down (Spaceman)
Space man came down (Spaceman)
Space man came down
Space man

Spaceman

Free Tempo

Words and Music by
David Brent

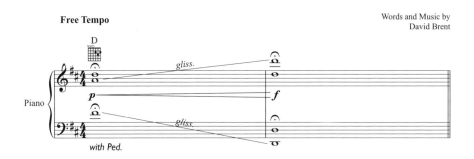

Piano

with Ped.

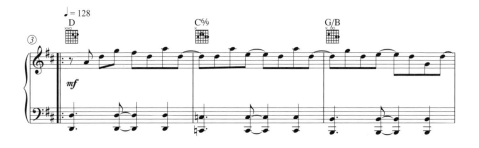

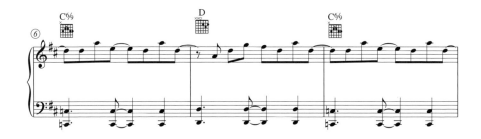

Equality Street

This is a political reggae song that imagines a street where people can live alongside each other in peace, whatever their race, sexuality or religion. "The Street" is obviously a metaphor for the whole world. (The streets I've known in real life, where people have been thrown together like this often create a lot of tension. But not in this song.)

It's also very informative, particularly the rap, which points out that dwarves are a lot heavier than you'd imagine when you try to actually pick one up. I was very surprised. I can only imagine they have a slightly higher density, but I couldn't find any information on it and I didn't want to actually ask one in case they were a bit sensitive about the whole subject. I care about people's feelings, however short they are. That's equality.

Equality Street

Let me take you down equality street
You never know da people you meet
At the end of da street is a golden gate
It let in love, it don't let in hate, no

Walk with me down equality street
Do unto others and life is sweet
Books have no covers, just look right in
You're judged by your words not da
colour of your skin, oh...

Deyo deyo deyo me say deyo
Biddly biddly biddly biddly biddly biddly bong yo

Yo, I'm like John Lennon
Except I DO imagine there's a heaven
Somewhere everyone is welcome all
my multicultural brethren
Where hate is outdated – Today
Love's the word
Even for people from Luxembourg
Well maybe like some other
countries that you might ignore
Tonga! Never thought of in my life before
But if I met a guy from Tonga then
we'd stop and we'd speak

In fluent Tongalese on Equality Street, Yep
Acceptance
See that Kenyan guy with mental eyes
He might be totally normal; you can't generalise
Black people aren't crazy
Fat people aren't lazy
And dwarves aren't babies
You can't just pick 'em up
They got rights
And anyway don't assume you could
They're not light
I learnt the hard way don't give a damn if
You're Russian or you're Spanish
We're comrades, compadres
You could be a half gay woman with a dark face
One leg, no legs! Long as you got a
heart, hey – transgender, gay,
straight, lesbians, whatever,
whoever, hey mate let's be friends,
but just friends. I want you to be
where you're properly free
obviously yes equality street,
believe.
You know the deal there, everything
is real fair
Take a ride on my equal opportunity
wheelchair
Yeah!

Come with me down equality street
You never know da people you meet
At the end of da street is a golden gate
It let in love, it don't let in hate, no
Equality Street
Equality Street
Equality Street
Biddly biddly biddly biddly biddly biddly bong, sweet!

EQUALITY STREET

Equality Street

Words and Music by David Brent
Rap by Dom Johnson

- en gate,___ it let in love,___ it don't let in hate,___ no.

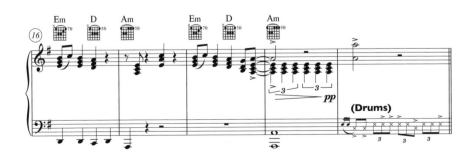

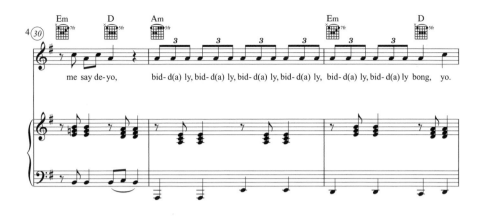

me say de-yo, bid-d(a) ly, bid-d(a) ly, bid-d(a) ly, bid-d(a) ly, bid-d(a) ly, bid-d(a) ly bong, yo.

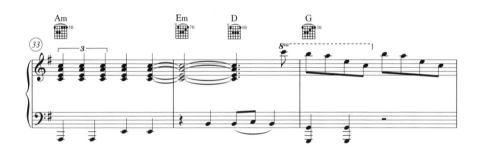

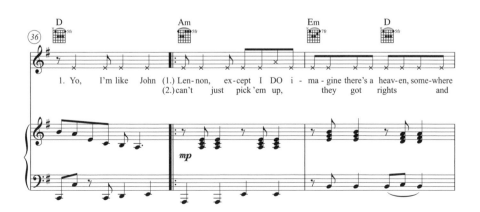

1. Yo, I'm like John (1.) Len-non, ex-cept I DO i-ma-gine there's a heav-en, some-where
(2.) can't just pick 'em up, they got rights and

life be-fore, but if I met a guy from Ton-ga then we'd stop and we'd speak in
as you got a heart, hey, trans-gen-der, gay, straight, les - bi-ans, what-

flu-ent Ton-ga-lese on e-qual-i-ty street. Yep, ac-cept-ance. See that
e - ver, who-e-ver, hey, mate, let's be friends- but just friends. I want you to

Ken-yan guy with men-tal eyes He might be to-tal-ly nor-mal you can't gen'ral-ise.
be where you're pro-per-ly free, ob-vi-ous-ly, yes, e-qual-i-ty street, be-lieve.

157

Ain't No Trouble

This is a calypso-funk fusion. Very few singer-songwriters attempt songs like this because they don't know how to put meaningful lyrics to such funky music. I'm the opposite. I sometimes put in too much meaning and get too funky, if anything. But I think I've got everything just right here.

It's sung through the eyes of an old rasta who doesn't care what happens to him as long as he's still got his woman. I originally wrote it for that guy who invented Reggae Reggae Sauce on *Dragons' Den,* but he wasn't interested. His condiment business is doing well and he seems to have left music behind him. Shame. His loss.

Dom does a cool rap on it though, which is great. I thought it would be good for him to do some limbo on stage to really bring it to life, but he said he can't limbo. I find that hard to believe, but I didn't want to push it in case he was just embarrassed to take his shirt off or something.

Ain't No Trouble

I can work all day just to earn a dollar
I can break my bones you never hear me holler
I can lose my home I'm kick out in the street
If my baby's by my side then life is sweet

Ain't no Trouble like trouble
when you lose the one you love
Ain't no Trouble like trouble
when you lose the one you love
Ain't no Trouble like the trouble
when you lose the one you love
Ain't no Trouble like trouble when
you lose the one you love

You can take my eyes Lord,
Leave me blind
You can make me lame Lord
I'm sit on my behind
And I still won't beg Lord
And I'm no hero
If my baby's by my side Lord
You've taken zero

Ain't no Trouble like trouble when
you lose the one you love
Ain't no Trouble like trouble when
you lose the one you love
Ain't no Trouble like the trouble
when you lose the one you love
Ain't no Trouble like trouble when
you lose the one you love

I could lose my job

But it'll be fine cos I could still find
the odd snob to rob

I could get chucked out

Of my mum's house but it could be
fun sleeping rough when the sun's
out

I could lose my voice

But I'd manage to still do some
sick rhyme damage with sign
language

Take what's mine

Almost anything, Xbox, wedding
ring, fish tank, terrapin. Poke me
in the eyeball pull out a gun, say
something spiteful about my mum,
tease my dog so he doesn't even
know it by going to throw a bone but
just pretending to throw it
Make death threats yeah and I have
to guess where, then when I get
there pull out my chest hair, head
butt me in the nuts if you want,
coz ain't no trouble like
losing the one you love.
Come on.

Ain't no Trouble like trouble when
you lose the one you love

Ain't no Trouble like trouble when
you lose the one you love
Ain't no Trouble like the trouble when
you lose the one you love
Ain't no Trouble like trouble when
you lose the one you love

And when I'm old and slow and grey
I forget me name, forget what day,
then I see this face and she smiles
at me. If I died right then Lord
I'd be happy
Cos ain't no trouble like trouble
when you lose the one you love
Ain't no trouble like trouble
when you lose the one you love
Ain't no trouble like the trouble when
you lose the one you love
Ain't no trouble like trouble
when you lose the one you love

Oh oh oh oh oh
Oh oh oh oh oh
Oh oh oh oh oh
Oh oh oh oh oh

Ain't No Trouble

Words and Music by David Brent
Rap by Dom Johnson

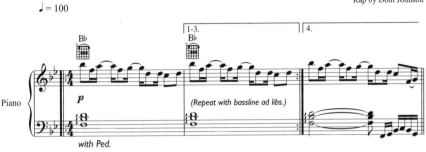

2 (10)

break my_ bones, you nev-ver hear_me hol ler, I can lose my_ home, I'm
make me_ lame, Lord, I'm sit on my_ be - hind, and I still won't beg, Lord, and

Bb   Gm   Eb   F   Bb   Gm

(13)

kick out in_ the street, if my bab-y's by my side_ then life is_sweet.⎫ Ain't no
I'm_ no_ hero, if my bab-y's by my side_ Lord, you've taken on_ zero.⎭

Eb   F   Bb   Gm   Eb   F

(16)

troub-le like_ troub-le when you lose the one_ you love, ain't no troub-le like_ troub-le when you

Bb   Gm   Eb   F   Bb   Gm

mf

166

Electricity

This is the most recent song I've written. It's sort of a homage to one of my favourite bands – Coldplay. It's about ordinary everyday things being magical in their own way. I guess that's what Chris Martin and I have in common, too. Just ordinary guys making inspirational works of art. He probably gets a lot more help and input from his band than I do, but that doesn't mean I'm more talented than him. No way.

Electricity

I was looking up to heaven
It was right under my nose
I had travelled many light years
It was right across the road.
A billion trillion grains of stardust
Floating round in space
Two of them collided in an ordinary place
We are electricity
We will never die
We'll just burn and burst and return to the sky
(Oh woah x6)
This world can't contain you
Gravity won't restrain you
Fly with me
High with me, high
We are electricity
We will never die
We'll just burn and burst and return to the sky
(Oh woah x6)

We are electricity, the universe reflects in you and me
We're electricity, the universe reflected
We are electricity, the universe reflects in you and me,
We're electricity just when I least expected

We are electricity, the universe reflects in you and me
We're electricity just when I least expected

Electricity

Words and Music by
David Brent

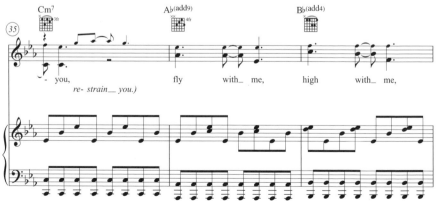

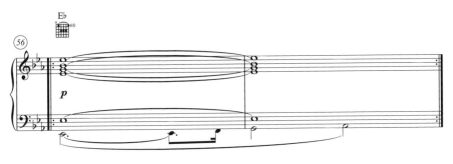

(Repeat x 3)

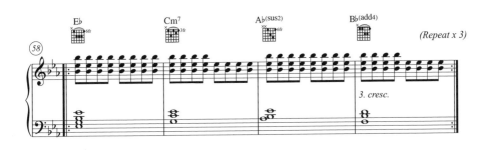

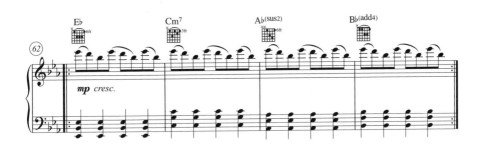

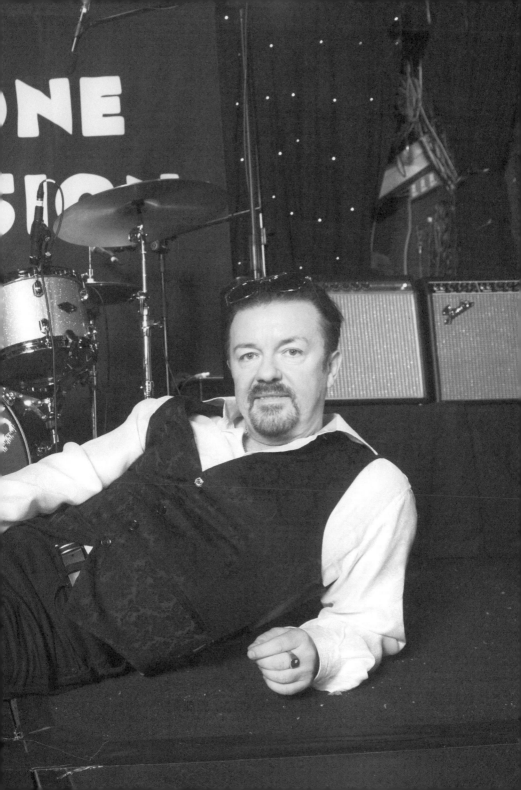

Credits

Ooh La La
Written by David Brent

Native American
Written by David Brent

Lonely Cowboy
Written by David Brent

Freelove Freeway
Written by David Brent

Life on the Road
Written by David Brent

Slough
Written by David Brent

Thanks Fuck It's Friday
Written by David Brent

Lady Gypsy
Written by David Brent

Please Don't Make Fun of the Disableds
Written by David Brent

Paris Nights
Written by David Brent

Don't Cry It's Christmas
Written by David Brent

Spaceman
Written by David Brent

Equality Street
Written by David Brent

Ain't No Trouble
Written by David Brent

Electricity
Written by David Brent

All the best
David Brent

David Brent
& Foregone Conclusion
LIFE ON THE ROAD

ALBUM OUT NOW

Featuring songs from the film, including the David Brent classics "Freelove Freeway" and "Equality Street".